YOU MUST REMEMBER THIS

1963

MILESTONES, MEMORIES,
TRIVIA AND FACTS, NEWS EVENTS,
PROMINENT PERSONALITIES &
SPORTS HIGHLIGHTS OF THE YEAR

TO: Leif

FROM: Aunt Cathy

MESSAGE: 1963 - the year
I was born!

*selected and researched
by
mary a. pradt*

WARNER Ⓦ TREASURES™

PUBLISHED BY WARNER BOOKS

A TIME WARNER COMPANY

COPYRIGHT ©1995
by Mary A. Pradt
All Rights Reserved.

Warner Books, Inc.
1271 Avenue of the Americas
New York, New York 10020

Warner Treasures is a
trademark of Warner Books, Inc.

A Time Warner Company

DESIGN:
CAROL BOKUNIEWICZ DESIGN
PRINTED IN SINGAPORE
FIRST PRINTING : MAY 1995
10 9 8 7 6 5 4 3 2 1
ISBN : 0-446-91039-2

November 22, 1963, 12:31 P.M. CST — President John F. Kennedy, Jr., the 35th American president, was shot to death in a motorcade in Dallas, TX. Jacqueline was beside him when the bullets flew. JFK was pronounced dead at Parkland Hospital within half an hour. At 2:15 P.M. the suspected assassin, Lee Harvey Oswald, was captured in a movie theater. At 2:38 P.M., aboard Air Force One, with federal judge Sarah T. Hughes presiding, Lyndon Baines Johnson took the oath of office; Lady Bird Johnson and a stunned and still bloodstained Jacqueline Kennedy were on either side. On November 24, Oswald, the accused assassin, was gunned down by Jack Ruby in a Dallas police building, and the event was caught on film for posterity. On November 25, the slain president was laid to rest in Washington. Just before the funeral ended, Mrs. Kennedy, a grieving and majestic Madonna veiled in black, placed an "Eternal Flame" at the head of the president's grave at Arlington.

Said Chief Justice Earl Warren, who would head the investigation into the assassination, "We can all be better Americans because John Fitzgerald Kennedy has passed our way."

On August 28 one hundred years after Emancipation, at least 200,000 blacks and whites assembled for the largest civil rights demonstration to date, the

march on washington.

newsreel

dr. martin luther king, jr., spoke: "I have a dream that one day this nation will rise up and live out the true meaning of its creed: 'We hold these truths to be self-evident, that all men are created equal.'" King's speech concluded with reference to the dream of being "Free at last, free at last; thank God Almighty, we are free at last." Among those at the Mall were: Roy Wilkins, John Lewis, Bob Dylan, Joan Baez, Jackie Robinson, Peter, Paul & Mary, and Josephine Baker.

It was a year of earthshaking and recordbreaking news and events, literally and metaphorically. An earthquake in Skopje, Yugoslavia, killed over 1,000, and Britain suffered the worst winter cold since 1740.

headlines

international

Kennedy visited the Berlin Wall on June 26, 1963, while **the cold war** raged. The phrase "Ich bin ein Berliner" was etched into our memory.

The U.S. and USSR agreed to communicate directly in the case of impending nuclear war—a catastrophe suggested by the book *Fail-Safe*. A nuclear test-ban treaty was finally signed.

4

the profumo affair

brought down John Dennis Profumo, the British war minister, and threatened Harold Macmillan's Tory government. The very-married Profumo was introduced to call girl Christine Keeler. It was the sort of thing that scandalized and fascinated both British and American audiences.

It was a big year for espionage and scandal.

VALENTINA TERESHKOVA BECAME THE WORLD'S FIRST SPACEWOMAN ON JUNE 16, ABOARD THE *VOSTOK VI*.

The New York City newspaper strike ended on April 1; nine dailies had been off the stands since December 8, 1962.

playboy reached the 2-million point in circulation. It was the epitome of the Good Life for most men.

frank sinatra, jr.,

was kidnapped from Lake Tahoe in December. He was ransomed for $240,000 by Sinatra, Sr.

cultural
milestones

POLAROID INTRODUCED THE FIRST 60-SECOND COLOR PRINT.

For the first time, a majority of Americans of college age were enrolled in institutions of higher learning.

'63

7

There were more than 50 million TV households in America. More than 91 percent of homes had sets. Only about 2 percent were color sets.

television

top-rated shows of the 1963 fall season:

1. "The Beverly Hillbillies" (CBS)

2. "Bonanza" (NBC)

3. "The Dick Van Dyke Show" (CBS)

4. "Petticoat Junction" (CBS)

5. "The Andy Griffith Show" (CBS)

6. "The Lucy Show" (CBS)

7. "Candid Camera" (CBS)

8. "The Ed Sullivan Show" (CBS)

9. "The Danny Thomas Show" (CBS)

10. "My Favorite Martian" (CBS)

casper the Friendly Ghost got his own Saturday morning TV show, "The New Casper Cartoon Show," on ABC at 11 A.M. Casper had been seen on the tube since 1953, in a syndicated series of 6 1/2 minute theatrical cartoons.

'63

milestones

divorce & wedding

Nelson Rockefeller, a potential presidential candidate, divorced his wife of 31 years and married **Margaretta Fitler Murphy,** a divorcee, on May 4 in Pocantico Hills, NY. Republican leaders differed on the impact this would have on a run for the top office.

D E A T H S

Robert Frost,
four-time Pulitzer Prize winner, passed away in January at age 88. A line from his poem "Mending Wall" ("Something there is that doesn't love a wall") had come to be linked symbolically with the Berlin Wall.

Pope John XXIII
died on June 3 after a long struggle with cancer. He had convened the important ecumenical council Vatican II. His successor, Giovanni Battista Montini, was elected in one of the shortest papal conclaves ever; he took the name Paul II and soon reopened the Vatican Council.

Medgar Evers,
civil rights worker, was assassinated in Mississippi in June.

William Edward Burghardt DuBois,
father of African American intelligentsia and of African liberation, died at 95 and was buried in Ghana.

Edith Piaf,
"the Little Sparrow," died at 47. It was like the sound of "an April nightingale" said the avant-garde playwright **Jean Cocteau.** Seven hours later Cocteau himself was dead, at 74.

Aldous Huxley
died on November 22, 1963, as did the British Christian scholar and writer **C. S. Lewis.**

births

BOBBY BONILLA, Mets third baseman, was born on February 23.

JOHN STAMOS, actor and star of the hit series "Full House," was born on August 19.

MICHAEL JORDAN, basketball legend and star of the Chicago Bulls, was born on February 17. After conquering basketball, he decided to apply his boundless talents to professional baseball!

CHARLES BARKLEY, basketball player for the Phoenix Suns, was born on February 20.

JULIE KRONE, a jockey, was born on July 24.

JULIAN LENNON, a musician and son of the late John Lennon, was born on April 8.

WHITNEY HOUSTON, singer, made her debut on August 9. She is married to fellow crooner Bobby Brown.

TATUM O'NEAL, actress and daughter of actor Ryan O'Neal, was born on November 5. She later married and divorced tennis superstar John McEnroe.

HELEN HUNT, actress and star of the smash series "Mad About You," was born on June 15.

GEORGE MICHAEL, a British pop musician, was born on June 25. He first made the scene as one half of the pretty-boy duo Wham.

63

1. **sugar shack** Jimmy Gilmer and the Fireballs
2. **he's so fine** The Chiffons
3. **dominique** The Singing Nun
4. **hey paula** Paul and Paula
5. **my boyfriend's back** Angels
6. **blue velvet** Bobby Vinton
7. **sukiyaki** Kyu Sakamoto

hit music

8. **i will follow him** Little Peggy March
9. **fingertips part 2** Little Stevie Wonder
10. **walk like a man** Four Seasons

PEAKING AT #2, BUT IT TOOK ON A LIFE OF ITS OWN — *"LOUIE LOUIE"* BY **THE KINGSMEN.**

Other tunes that reached #1 on the charts included:
"I'm Leaving It All Up to You" (Dale and Grace)
"Surf City" (Jan and Dean)
"It's My Party (And I'll Cry if I Want To)" (Lesley Gore)
"Walk Right In" (Rooftop Singers)
"Our Day Will Come" (Ruby and the Romantics)

folkier material

was coming up fast. "Puff the Magic Dragon," by Peter, Paul, and Mary, was popular, as was "Blowin' In the Wind." The Village Stompers did "Washington Square." Trini Lopez covered "If I Had a Hammer."

"SURFIN' U.S.A." BY THE BEACH BOYS AND **"WIPE OUT"** BY THE SURFARIS WERE ALSO HITS.

fiction

1. **the shoes of the fisherman**
   morris l. west

2. **the group**
   mary mccarthy

3. **raise high the roof beam, carpenter
   and seymour — an introduction**
   j. d. salinger

4. **caravans**
   james a. michener

5. **elizabeth appleton**
   john o'hara

6. **grandmother and the priests**
   taylor caldwell

7. **city of night**
   john rechy
   *(This first novel shocked readers with its depiction
   of gay male lifestyles in the big city.)*

8. **the glass-blowers**
   daphne du maurier

9. **the sand pebbles**
   richard mckenna
   (Also a first novel, this one set in China in the 1920s.)

10. **the battle of the villa fiorita**
    rumer godden

JUST SHORT OF THE
TOP 10 IN SALES
WAS **IAN FLEMING**'S
*ON HER MAJESTY'S
SECRET SERVICE.*

books

nonfiction

1. **happiness is a warm puppy**
   charles m. schulz

2. **security is a thumb and a blanket**
   charles m. schulz

3. **j.f.k.: the man and the myth**
   victor lasky

4. **profiles in courage**
   inaugural edition
   john f. kennedy

5. **o ye jigs & juleps!**
   virginia cary hudson

6. **better homes and gardens**
   bread cook book

7. **the pillsbury family cook book**

8. **i owe russia $1200**
   bob hope

9. **heloise's housekeeping hints**

10. **better homes and gardens**
    baby book

Other important books were Sylvia Plath's *The Bell Jar* and Betty Friedan's enormously influential *The Feminine Mystique*.

15

Copr. © 1958, 1965 United Feature Syndicate, Inc.

'63

stan "the man" musial

played his last game for the St. Louis Cardinals, retiring at 42 to take an executive job with the club. Musial was a great hitter who played 22 years and set or tied dozens of major records.

John Pennel became the first person to pole vault 17 feet, reaching 17′ 3/4″ at a meet in Miami.

LITTLE LEAGUE BASEBALL'S CHAMPION-SHIP GAME WAS COVERED FOR THE FIRST TIME ON A NATIONAL TV NETWORK, ON ABC'S "WIDE WORLD OF SPORTS."

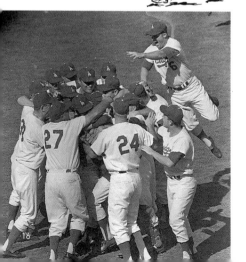

the l.a. dodgers

swept the New York Yankees in four games in the World Series. Pitcher Sandy Koufax set a new series record by striking out 15 players in the opening game.

Arnold Palmer was the leading money winner for the year in golf, earning $81,448.33.

james w. whittaker,

accompanied only by a Sherpa guide, became the first American to scale Mount Everest. A few weeks later, four more Americans climbed Everest, from the opposite side.

sports

The 47th annual Indy 500 was won by Parnelli Jones in 3 hours, 29 minutes, 35.40 seconds, at an average speed of 143 mph.

BOB COUSY, brilliant guard of the Boston Celtics, retired at 34, after leading the Celts to 5 straight NBA championships. The Celtics beat the Los Angeles Lakers 4 games to 2 in April.

box-office champs

1. *Cleopatra*
2. *The Longest Day*
3. *Irma La Douce*
4. *Lawrence of Arabia*
5. *How the West Was Won*
6. *Mutiny on the Bounty*
7. *Son of Flubber*
8. *To Kill a Mockingbird*
9. *Bye Bye Birdie*
10. *Come Blow Your Horn*

CLEOPATRA WAS INCREDIBLY EXPENSIVE TO MAKE. IT COST OVER $44 MILLION, BUT IT ONLY GROSSED $15,700,000, ALTHOUGH IT WAS THE TOP-EARNING FILM OF THE YEAR.

ACADEMY AWARD WINNERS
Best Picture went to **Tom Jones,** the Tony Richardson classic. Richardson directed and produced. **Sidney Poitier** was named Best Actor for *Lilies of the Field*, over Albert Finney for *Tom Jones*, Richard Harris in *This Sporting Life*, Rex Harrison in *Cleopatra*, and Paul Newman in *Hud*. **Patricia Neal** took Best Actress honors for her role in *Hud*, winning out over Leslie Caron in *The L-Shaped Room*, Shirley MacLaine in *Irma La Douce*, Rachel Roberts in *This Sporting Life*, and Natalie Wood in *Love with the Proper Stranger*. **Melvyn Douglas,** from *Hud*, won the Best Supporting Actor Oscar, and **Margaret Rutherford** was best supporting actress for her role in *The V.I.P.s*. **Tom Jones** and **How the West Was Won** received Best Screenplay Oscars. **Hud** and **Cleopatra** took cinematography honors, for black and white and color respectively. **Tom Jones** and **Irma La Douce** won scoring Oscars. The Best Song, however, was "Call Me Irresponsible," from **Papa's Delicate Condition** — music by James Van Heusen and lyrics by Sammy Cahn. Other nominated tunes were "Charade," "It's A Mad, Mad, Mad, Mad World," "More," from *Mondo Cane*, and "So Little Time." Federico Fellini's **8 1/2** was named Best Foreign Language Film.

top box-office stars

Doris Day	Elizabeth Taylor
John Wayne	Elvis Presley
Rock Hudson	Sandra Dee
Jack Lemmon	Paul Newman
Cary Grant	Jerry Lewis

It was the year of Alfred Hitchcock's *The Birds*, which won no Oscars, however.

movies

THIS WAS ALSO THE YEAR OF POLANSKI'S *KNIFE IN THE WATER*.

THE AVERAGE COST OF A MOVIE TICKET IN 1963 WAS 84.6 CENTS.

19

It was a banner year for the American car industry. Consumers were buying lavishly and actively. Production of passenger cars was up nearly 10 percent, to more than 7 million. Chevrolet dominated the bestselling models, with almost one third the industry's total production. One tabulation listed 334 different models. The top of the line, pricewise, was the Cadillac 75 limousine, at $9,939. Several carmakers got back into sponsoring competitive auto racing, a policy the Auto Manufacturers association

cars

had opposed. This meant that Ford, for example, supported stock-car events around the country and backed a team at the Indy 500. One novel development was the increasing popularity of hand-shifted transmissions. Four-speed manual transmissions operated by floor-mounted sticks made it possible to simulate the experience of driving a racing car.

The sleek **thunderbird** premiered, the coolest set of wheels since the '57 Chevy. With A/C and power windows, it was a car to covet in 1963. Collectors in the nineties still cherish their vintage T-Birds.

LEASING CARS WAS A GROWING TREND. COSTS WERE ABOUT $100–$200 A MONTH.

20

Double-Safety Brakes—self-adjusting, too

Bucket Seats, Console, Twin-Stick Floor Shift

Most miles per gallon in all Economy Events entered

Rambler American "440" Convertible. Power top is standard.

GO FOR FUN—SAVE A BUNDLE
(it's the Economy King with brand-new zing!)

TOP QUALITY AT AMERICA'S LOWEST PRICE!

Manufacturer's suggested retail price for the 1963 Rambler American "220" Two-Door Sedan. Optional equipment, transportation, state and local taxes, if any, extra.

$1846

This is the Rambler American "440" Convertible • This is the rakish, new beauty that gives a lift and a lilt to your spirits • This is the sporty stepper that you can own for fewer dollars than any other power-top convertible built in these United States • This is the eager-to-move fun car with a sweet-purring 125-horsepower Six, or you can have the extra zest of the 138-horsepower option • This is the sunshine version of the Rambler Americans that have won in every economy run entered with highest miles per gallon—an unmatched victory record • This is the smart one you can have with optional individually adjustable Reclining Bucket Seats, handsome and handy console, head-rests, exclusive Twin-Stick Floor Shift with Instant Overtake for exuberant sports-car action • This is the compact that's quality-built from its very core—and one reason why Rambler won MOTOR TREND MAGAZINE's coveted 1963 "Car of the Year" Award • Go for fun and save a bundle— see your Rambler dealer now • *American Motors—Dedicated to Excellence*

RAMBLER '63 WINNER OF MOTOR TREND AWARD CAR OF THE YEAR

Several different trends marked the fashion landscape. In *haute couture*, Chanel was named a "fashion immortal." Hot young designers included Rudi Gernreich of California, Pierre Cardin of Paris, and the English designer Mary Quant. One look was the sophisticated but sporty style borrowed from menswear and work clothes — i.e., **French peasant smocks, double-stitched workshirts,** and **low-slung pants.** Collegiate clothes for fall featured lots of **plaids, big checks,** and **camel.** The skirt length was exactly mid–knee; knee socks completed the look. Fake furs were big. Real fox and raccoon collars worked. Another popular look was **quasi-Bohemian,** rather like a Chelsea girl from London or an Actors Studio escapee from New York. This look was characterized by **the jumper, the trench coat,** and **turtleneck sweaters.** Sometimes patterns and colors were kookily combined. Lanky hair and startling makeup completed this look.

fashion

POPULAR FOOTWEAR INCLUDED **OXFORDS, GHILLIES,** AND **ALLIGATOR** OR **LIZARD LOW–HEELED SHOES. OPENBACKED SANDALS** AND **T-STRAPPED SHOES** FLOURISHED, TOO.

Evening clothes were dramatic and sirenlike, either evoking movie stars of the thirties and forties, or echoing Cleopatra in the *luxe* garments, accentuated with dramatic **kohl-lined eyes,** and **sphinx-like haircuts.**

Children's fashions began to attract important designers. Miniaturized versions of high fashion and kooky clothes appeared.

23

final
factoid

the limbo rock was an auxiliary twist craze, introduced by Chubby Checker, the father of the original twist. Other teen favorites were the dog, monkey, mashed potatoes, the slop, and the slurp.

archive photos: inside front cover, pages 1, 5, 6, 7, 11, 15, 17, 23, 25, inside back cover.

associated press: pages 2, 4, 16.

photofest: pages 8, 9, 10, 13, 18, 19.

original photography:
beth phillips: pages 13, 21, 22.

album cover:
courtesy of bob george/
the archive of contemporary music: page 13

photo research:
alice albert

coordination:
rustyn birch

design:
carol bokuniewicz design
mutsumi hyuga

'63